VERS ALOE

CW01261788

All too well & All the best

– eling . 24 xmas eve

VERS ALOE

DEMING HUANG

Overwhelm Press

CONTENTS

GHOST OF PEACH BLOSSOM LAND

Silver Spine

1

4

2

3

He was used to fusing with history at night. Maybe it was the news he listened to in the morning, a book he read in the afternoon, or someone he met for dinner in the evening. As long as his back was carefully landing on the mattress and his neck was meticulously embedded in the pillow. His soul would drift away from gravity, sometimes even to the moon. During his soul's escapade, he would always appear to be more frivolous than in the daylight. Like a wobbly dandelion with nothing to do, he was at home anywhere. In a barren desert he had seen a wrecked plane, large or small scorpion pincers and tails in the crevices of the fuselage and between the sand holes, he thought he saw scorpions flying in his vision, confused by the wind and sand. Until covered by a fierce thirst, the next second he was present in a juvenile reformatory in the early twentieth century. He was at a loss for tongues like an ornamental animal brought illegally into a foreign country. All he knew were the cold, eager, or threatening eyes of the youths. Fortunately, he was just a wild rootless soul, because the real world didn't really care much about him. Like the youths who surround him: they are banished from society, abandoned by the soil of habit. In this land of domesticated beasts, desire is the only nourishment that feeds their flesh and blood. Finally, in the den where he woke up from one of his dreams, his back was soaked with the sweat of the boy beside him, like a wet rose. He presses the boy away: he has completed the rite of passage into manhood. His eyes were no longer dazed: his fellow beasts who had once torn each other apart had taught him how to go out of his physical wakefulness and thus fly away. And so he flew, higher and higher, until his rakish flesh crashed into a room heavily like a sick plane.

1

4

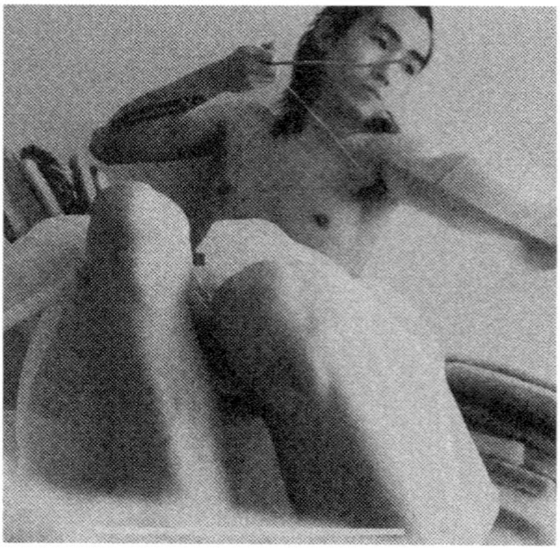

2

3

Parasites of the forest
may your bows and arrows never again be stained with blood!
Here the herbs and bushes are far curlier and more luxuriant than pubic
hair, like shining feathers. Perhaps burning cigarette ends can start a fire,
careful with your weapon. History proves that desire cannot be put off,
midnight pics cannot be burnt, only ideal love can be turned into ashes, literally.
And there are those who are cruising, morally, are defenceless.
A Rabbit God frowns.

And what about loneliness?
The night is young, and you scroll through your phone bitterly,
in your underwear waiting for something to happen,
a reason to trade a kiss, a cuddle, a war.
But what they see is another soul carrying a bow on a bare back,
in a room, with a bulge like an angry arrow, longing for fresh meat,
you'll get overwhelmed by the reward of great joys and regrets.
Be aware they may have a pillow fight inside your body;
you bleed, you smile.

And for these sickening ones
in a world of bows and arrows, I study you.
I will worship you, sabotage myself, salute you and spit on everyone.
Sailing away upon the violent waves, running in the summer gardens
of dog days, trying on random strangers' shoes.
We boycott!
For boys of your kind, for girls we kissed. For the namby-pamby, for the lost little chickens. For a celebration of chaotic energy, drinks for everybody and nobody
Because in the adventures of tops and bottoms, we re-experience the same things again and again in order to be different, honestly; stigma adapted
We, forever fabulous.

Hands on the keyboard, C-pop fills the ears.
The world's our oysters, darlin', no more fear.
And in your search history, our shadows shall meet.
Be warned!
All slain ghosts dance around the hunter:
when the sun is up you will become one of us.

Boy

1

4

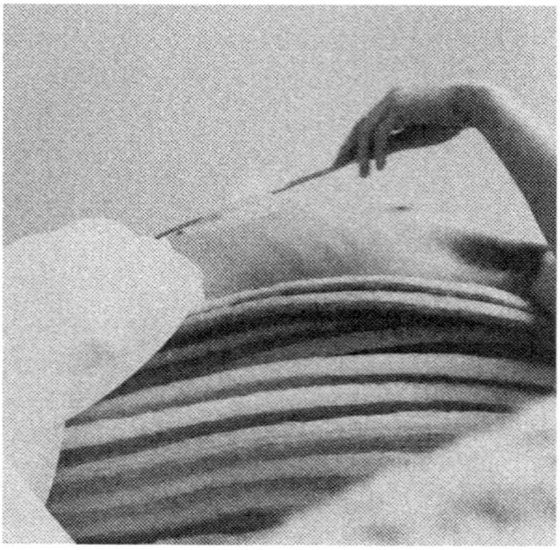

2

3

Boy, you laugh like you mean it.

If I am honest,
I am the worst person to fall in love with
and you are the best.

Perhaps you don't need earthly mortals... nor love.
Perhaps you're a ghost from another world, though
already you've broken into my kingdom in full fury.

... Cedar over a bed of daises

Leaving a collapsed land, I slept fitfully.
Two islands confronting each other:
you make me my own enemy.

I inject condemnation and pareidolia for hypnosis to fall asleep at night.
And stimulate my body with fairytales and horrifying speculations in the dark—
your name feeds a charm of witchcraft that curses me.

Even worse, my finger missed yours.

You're the three witches. If not
You're the Trinity. When you no longer hold my blurry hand—
I'm invisible in your inbox.

Boy, you left like you meant it.

i

The birth of a hunter is the death of a herd of prey. He walks into the crowd with a battle-scarred body and tangible results, ready to trade, but the market price is always uncertain. To add insult to injury, he had to go to the black market for safety reasons. The stall is full of cheap torsos, drug dealers, cryptic symbols and emojis, genuine or pirated—drawn at his own risk. Funny how the malediction is 'Masc 4 Masc', to a passage packed with Polari, anonymous accounts, and offers by the masked. Sprouting, the hunting instinct in the dark forest is an awakening of self-consciousness.

ii

There are motley sales in the arcades, and he has coins and a folded towel like an animal in his hands. Having flicked through bizarre and alien anthologies, from the basics of vanilla flavours to a group activity that tastes of leather with musk, he discovers who he can be in his desire. Race, age and looks are bargaining chips, and in this gamble, he loses track of what he sought since childhood. In exchange, he earned blue pills and a radar for secret gatherings. The ephemeral joy and suffering is experimentation in an effort to bring lives to life.

iii

In the end, the hunter devoted himself to Saint Twink, like how parents package their children to fit their whims. Meanwhile, all sorts of plants and trees grow into a dense forest of mutual torment. The lowest beings learn to wait in the darkness, lying dormant, gnawing on decaying bodies, and love at their own expense. The galaxy is impressed by this unrelenting energy and decides to descend as sensual and infected spores. The deaths of outsiders make the universe shake. Do not fear ghostly possession—it serves healing recuperation. Passing is simply becoming.

Go then: like how you made Mother cry.
Nothing in the world can stop you now. We've played all our cards.
Here, take these fables and fairy tales; they'll come in handy,
    At your lowest battle with self-sabotage.
    Stand still after one thousand and one nights, clinging to see another day of light.
Please, the sail is on: remember when you found the pretty box with dead flowers,
    We'll know why the ocean is blue—
    And nothing can kill us anymore.

ODE ON TOPOPHILIA

Cruising over
spoilt bones, we curate
Whatever modern thingamajigs display
(Have I told you) I get mesmerised by the bushes

Woods aren't
for leisure, harsh nettle bites
Up, up!
Hansel and Gretel had their lessons (too easy)

Contemporaries old
forest taste, new
Too fashionable
(For that matter) we fucked nature at a very young age

[Together] HERE IS THE LAND.
HERE IS WHERE THE OBJECT ENTANGLES US

ONLY FOOLS DESPAIR

Two angels falling into a bed of whites,
Hit up and down,
Of all genders, glamour everywhere.

In-between their play,
One sheds a tear, the eye arrests it, red but fine
The other commuted back to the edge of romance, searched & said:

'Need to go. To get to work!'
This time words enfold them with material air,
It's lenient to have a psyche, to go deeper with the darkness.

Rest in a limbo of nature,
They accept the ebbs and flows. Out of the blue, a passing wind whispered to the wings:
'I'm pretty sure you are sun-kissed and worth a world of wine.'

So the fishes' gills crushed, at some point I lost
that one possibility of breathing, the remaining
active material is mixed and stirred, hydrating
isolated in vacuum, comes with grease, bodily
up and down and then back and forth, goodies
suffocated, divided, oxygenated, safely stored
sensitive, your eyes gently shatter, butterfly-ish
my kingdom drowned in ruins, for your use only

FALL HARD, FALL FAST

The time you drove me back from the city to Wheelers Hill
We had gotten out from the Laneway festival with your friends
Under the alert eye of seagulls everywhere, you got distracted
By the youth and the pumping night in euphoria, you pilot
And merge the car into a reflective verge on a safety island. It was hectic.

With you, it all starts with being enthralled by this crush at the first sign
Going on through one more accident after another, clumsy little you
Often preoccupied with other infatuation, miles away. And
After witnessing another screw-around, clumsy belittling me
Finally waking up, mesmerised by the 5D views, wheels up.

The memory of our tumble road trips and St Kilda's sea breeze
All crashed into a nebulous glow with my nineteen years.

VERSE ON A VANISHING ACT (AS READ BUT NO REPLY)

another comet hit the earth, and i
joined my dinosaurs in being helplessly
        exterminated. Craving for centuries
to be dug up and exhibited (eventually)
if you could see my desperate eyes
        yes, i'd like you to cry—
cry until you dry. Capitalism
lacks our feelings

you said
you are in my world
        (in that way) i had entered
if only (that worked)
i want to be a cold merchant
        (like you are), sell me (to you)
clock-haunted silence, opening an end
to the waiting of Godot

praying is the second child
of inability, and i'll learn
        to grow up on my own
after being worn down by oxygen, no more use
a misty war broke a user's server: all data lost
        you suggested: i must put myself first
in that (lower) case, who else will
text you (like i can)? to be continued…

THREE DESIRING-MACHINES

Eros

jar of fruits
one that has been frightfully mashed,
indistinguishable you and me,
spices and the bittersweet, harder.

hurts all over
waiting to be consumed,
but soon we start from scratch,
ready for absorption and sharing.

exile is jail
airtight by force, memory squeezed
and popped, exert before best-before bursts out.
*I'm eating my feelings. Will my stomach digest better this time?

Orpheus

impossible to let go
even if you've been gone so long
so long. Demolishing all the walls. Hence alone.

turn on the music
it ought to be unbounded
brighten up a way out. Yet the sun is behind the fence.

scrying, seeking, and worshipping your echo
crystal clear. Remembering washes me soft
lingering voidness retraces some warmth.

see, I'm barely hanging on. As all tumbles
into dense and crimped tribulations
would you come home and fold me right—

Aphrodite

i am as broken as i can be
the more pieces I become
the better the chance of you picking me up—
stepped over by all the Queen's horses
feeling our bodies scatter over
crippling songs and verses now but curses—
i'm always at your service—oh no
i mean, we are here, or almost at your hand
look down, please knees
complete this solitude, glow job
off and on, sporadically
moments sweeter than gold, colder than death
with many-mes under one
barefoot, defeated, all shivering.

Earlier That Day

You've shut down last night's rain, and don't need this overdue coolness anymore
You roll up linen sleeves, and walk into fresh summer with funky shining sunglasses
And just like the change of season, you take off our ties and shop for new accessories

From the dated canal to the weekend markets, jobs and sunbeams make you anxious
It would help if you had a hat—but you forget you've got a new hairdo. So precious.
It's not too long, not too short, not too cheap, not too expensive, but the finger lingers

Such a contradictory day. You think to yourself and remember to close the windows tonight.

Later That Night

I've been left halfway across a savage desert, wandering barefoot, shoes stolen
Hallucinations appear when searching for an oasis, or even grander, a vending machine
A cactus pierces a paperback calendar and every day becomes a repeat of the sandstorm
There is no more life to look forward to. Despair sets in and all hopes end up in a landfill
Feeling the rave party turn into a mirage, I'd gladly run to it. I'm Lola running for my aching
Yearningly scorpion-crawling halophyte that has travelled from the sea searching for a cavity

Such a big downfall for my little stage. Stab me the way you snubbed me and let me be
stubbornly salty.

IS HUNTING AND FORAGING AN INSTINCT LEFT FROM HUMAN EVOLUTION OR IS IT A SKILL LEARNED BY AN UNSPEAKABLE FORCE IN THE SOCIAL JUNGLE?

the doors don't lock
like a new domestic pet
intruding into the jungle party of testosterone
they looked at me in echelon
ripples pull soiled land inwards
with eyes that stripped me naked as Styrofoam
and devoured me in trancelike hospitality
'you are wild and free now.
here, you don't need a master.
here, you can be a master,'
a volcano in the next cubicle erupted
overwhelmed in exuberant waves and lava
'or be my favourite of the day'
it turns out that predators
are always minimal and stay ready
communicate with body language only
a fleeting burst of pouncing their aims
so I dusted off civilisation
and began seeking my prey
pray that my timidity goes away, swallowed
no locust dares to utter a sound, shallow
just their instinct continues to scramble
worries were taken care of
this path to immortality
is not only a path of restraint
and tortoise breath, ethological
but also a good way to savour every magical
moment of consuming our body and soul
take a dip and sip on the queer's share
hold me tight, loosen me up
like the way tides follow the moon in time
during all the silent intervals
landslides a tsunami called normalcy
defying all gravity
coming to destroy
while the abnormal ones
wait for one chance
it turns back
knocks the basin over
slash—cuts the surface
from that day onwards
all sea was scarred

SAUNA SONNETS

A Greedy Life

Its harvest of voyeurism haunts us, with a trident of our own design,
Inside the rubbers and the sweet wrappers, a compass leads us down lost ways,
Enmeshed, cold, damp ceramic infrastructures shore up our patience,
Like ferns, like owls, we cling to this entanglement. HAHA a diva down
To misfortunes, on schadenfreude's prowl. Dangers soak in lustful ways,
Rich, thick with loads of glue that sticks to belly buttons, whilst
Sprinkles from a functioning nozzle sanitise and sensitise our farewell chokehold kiss.
The elusive shadow of physicality and knowledge follows lost patterns,
As we swing and hesitate in the direction of each other's eyes.
I hold my breath as you play with my skin and sins. Scissors, paper, stone,
We confess the oath under the flashing traffic lights, lustful in patterns
Of red, amber, green. My apple pops as Adam bulks up my little needs,
At the immersive playfield for predatory. This arena is Mount Olympus, where the faggots
Climb on one and all in a *pragmatic and kinetic* way. Desire can map us to utopia.

It's Sexy

when the threshold is heated, you walk in as Our Lady of the Flowers
locked and curtained with blatant ocean ballads, melodrama
it's sexy: when everyone is queuing for sling goodies to let loose
you rock the theme park alone. An old world sparrow gliding through a pack
of Newfoundland dogs. It's not sexy that someone jumps to a conclusion before
anyone makes a move abusing improvised jazz with their rough hands and balmy lips.
I wish the Discovery channel could potentially touch and spy on them
moreover, no fun when the torch hits; the ground-feast explodes in HD
in a blink of an eye, diplomatic protocol creeps in when modern affairs occur in conflict,
good deal. A bro in a booth or hubby in the hot tub, this universal exposition will not burn
off. It's divine when we transform back to teenage mall-rats, craving for nectar and pollen
so many and most of the time so few, us nasty bees busy checking on nothing
in a beehive of unfulfilled holes with unfertilised eggs, great tragedy!
Searching for the miraculous ending, nature is only a shower away.

Happy Family

Daddy is hurting me as he pushes pleasure into my miserable consciousness, a psychedelic field he is running on with the help of mutual hypnosis, I work my ass off for this proposition That I am performing a bad son and a good wife. This lousy brat is growing up to be a good wife. She carries a century of human needs, for that, suffers from the domestic to the Black Hole of life. You like that, huh? Daddy breaks the fourth wall while I'm concentrating on the ceiling light, which reminds me of a kumquat. Father's favourite fruit. To correspond I want to spill something, but I won't say anything. Being silent is a woman's first course and I'm still preparing for my society debut. A ground speech that begins with eyes meeting and Finish with a smelly empty room. Daddy, would you pick me as your only star that matters tonight? Mesmerising me with your veiny torso with a steely voice, enduring uncut gem, Daddy, does my pretence make you proud now? Or I shall put your presence into one of my artisanal pieces: a collection of intense impulse that a body had experienced, with an aura of Top notes of foam-party mixed occasionally with stolen poppers, Mediterranean bergamot oil, sweat sun-glared their face, and shoots spectacular loads on a portrait with ghost genes.

Second Shower

'No kiss,' he confessed. Skin wrenches by the sweat of desire. Shivering & ached.
'Turn around,' he ordered. No sunlight penetrates this cloistered pod of the nocturnal.
'Too intense?' he asked. The tenderness of a stranger often spins me soft.
'Second shower!' another busy hunting fellow explorer pays minor thought, calculating
Spots me in a hurry, no shame, but several unwanted speculations
As though I'm now used and sorted, a fallen fruit landed on bare ground, free for all
I shall soon become rotten, perhaps, if the night is still young and yearning
Or I should be a replica of others, as ever, learning to be verisimilitudinous
In this painting of circles and sirens, I'm frowning for attention.
And for the annotation of manhood, our greasy troubles get washed off in the shower
The sinking sins drain well. Thus, in steam, I recalled limbs without deodorant.
The water is adequately hot; a study of boiling. Like, solo ploughing cultivating soils
Then my roommates of many talents are gathering at an ungodly hour, a baptism
All confide in me, planting me, back and forth, all because of a single soaked seed.

Rabbit Hole (Orgasm)

Vicissitudes in   one touch
we are
taking off our girdle of jealousy
we are
substantial voidness
which is
a dancing etiquette for
parades of endorphins
OH YES YES YES
moan in   and   out
At the till
we are fully dressed again
Until
you lay your towel on my tail again—

The Glimpse of Artemis

Maybe the other bodies no longer matter, nor does the outer space & many eyes gazing.
His hands are exquisite sexual comforts he acquires. A love song dripping down on himself
We are all sheer volume. That is what I composed anyway. While I'm checking him out—
someone dry and preserved is perhaps also painting me into such bathing scenes, liquids
Follow my face going down to my chest, and the rest is covered and tucked in cheap towels is
it mine or his? A question indeed. Like this one: why this sculpture keeps taking showers
As if London hasn't had enough rain already. Was he from a tropical land such as I am?
Tepid streams should stick together. Imagining we eventually become one silver wave
swallowing up the dirt of cities, unwelcoming skin contacts that are gesture without consent
Is that why he depicted himself in the water? To wash away the filthy speculations of being
accessible, for a pillar of salt he reforms and serves. Tender, timid as a shy undermined river
he resembles a Greek myth. Hoping, after this, he will be uncontaminated. Nymph-free.
Maybe he doesn't care about being echoed and desired. He expected to be clean, warm &
private in the womb. Where every place is safe. That everything will turn out just all right.

Chances Are

before I tore apart, you
come along with your bells
on and drop your banana key chain
on the sticky table. Waiting for you
—smelling like chlorine, so wet, but you
look like a movie star—so hot. The day
Achilles flicked the fruits in the air, used, out
so I pass the bench where we see, listen, and feel
so I go on and toss a coin to make a wish. A dream. In
the picture of your old room the snow covers yesteryears and
we would be kids again. Tropical pop and red bean puff, taste innocent. There won't
be one single destructive emotion involved. We kissed and
kissed till we both turned into a thousand sunburnt
muggy sultry pieces (that would be a fine thing).

Trash Talking

A: If I didn't spend all this time watching porn, I might be a minister already.
B: I'm pretty sure the minister watches porn too. Like, shitloads.
A: No shit. Not as much as me, tho.
B: Not as good as you, too.
I listen as I make notes. One day, I might be a minister for these two—
This public servant is a gay porn lover. And now he's aroused (power!) and bared.
Think of Foucault, in the group's centre—a reality show star in heterotopia—panopticon.
I wonder if my 10% incomprehensible-ness is a fist of obscurity for others here, punishing.
Look, A & B start to make out after blocking out my eager-to-please eye contact, I'm out.
Think of Rimbaud; I should put on my armour of ego, be my only fan.
Bad timing. It's too late as my bones don't have any more lubricants. And so,
I polished my cabinet avowed to eliminate phantasms and simulacra in the cave of fandom.
Bear enough suffering, I dress & am ready to go out as a minister. A kingdom of watching.
At times when nothing happens, I construct abstracted reverie. Masturbating, too.

Night Of Fickle

I see we meet again at last.
'Again' had been sacrificed and faded because of the long separation in between.
It still makes me feel like a kid who's just met and can't wait to impress his new friend. Pulling out all his latest treats and greatest gadgets and laying them out one by one, cute. Story goes on, and then you'd reciprocate; we'd play house, do chores together.
Mopping the floor impeccably, washing off filthy sheets and putting on the new dream.
You admit you didn't want to keep on being exiled, looking for a break in the weight of life.
I propose you deserve all the lightsome things and share games and movies I dig recently.
I suggest playing and watching them with you, but secretly reconsider that I'm not worthy.
Will I be your responsibility or embarrassment, happy and sad for me alone, or do you care?
I never meant to bother you, yet your presence is an ache I can't ignore or leave behind.
I understand you want to run away, for I stuffed you with what I thought you wanted.
And what is unloved is burdened, and what is wanted is not always needed.
And finally, rightfully so, I wake up alone once again. Outside, the sun is vigilantly bright.

Three Fashionable Boyfriends

Trench coats, oversized jackets & pullovers—they took them all off—we put them all on
everyone witnessing, the beginning of one shop is
the breaking down of another. Layer after layer
the tourists learn to pack up their feelings
and belongings before they leave, four seasons in one day. From a boy to a man
all filthy roads outside become opulent runways
and it is compulsory to make performance art about it
partially zooming in on the eyes of the passengers
in the rear-view mirror, and you will see
its staged gestures of vanity—carefully curated
a psychological rehearsal before the haggle
after leaving the labyrinth, I took the ball
of thread given by Ariadne and waited for
Theseus to save me in his phone.

• • •

Perhaps because the souls of the seven young men
and the seven maidens were attached, stitched
to his subjected body, gifting him with several personas. Layer after layer
the representative ones were a sound engineer, an NHS nurse, a forensic scientist
and a couple (a maths teacher married to a legal notary for seven years
visiting from a city outside Paris). They kept mending
and replacing my unicorn-party-punctured soul
and torn clothes, maintaining a weary shame
I preserved and continued to bite on for days
wandering in front of the same shop windows
same foggy air, same birthday present, same nocturnal animals, creeping in fragments
of hazy landscapes that city dwellers have never seen. We were able to glimpse a way
out of a few blurred meanings. In our weekly repeated movements, slow and deep
of a fashionable split second. Love me longer or love me not.

• • •

Is the bus still running? Are you going South or West? I am tired as hell
I still haven't sent off my first message. I must not wait for his ghost ship any longer
in the Aegean Sea; no signal on this island. Not a man, not a god. Layer after layer
minding and sensing my drained body squirming in my red pullover. Albeit,
my knee is bleeding and pants need washing, sucked at life is intense
nonstop friction. Still, I found a bottle of champagne to ease the tension. For instance,
the fabric I am in smelled like a mix of rosehip and coffee grounds—delicious skin—
and is as different as twink and daddy; compared to disinfectant wipes and poppers
it may only take seven years to cast the change in two roles, though
it can also wear away the texture of the mind overnight—never underestimate the power of
a raging sex awakening. So is the end-of-season clearance; it can be very ugly icily observing
where my clothes and bus seat upholstery rub against each other, it gets kinky hot. Sea island
cotton and polyester indulge in an impulsive sex encounter, electric,
as a fashion shot of passengers' faces is completed at the final stop—flushed & flashed!

GENTS

Of course,
this charming man reveals his violence
in his crafted words held by mighty hands
pulls me forward, then pushes down

So,
that is how it must feel to be a bad bitch
to go from a garden plant to conquer a continent
the danger of contagion brings a thrill of extinction

Maybe,
I miss the perfect geometry
in which I was safe and babied. If only his character
stayed at 'first impression' and less 'natural aggression'

A stranger estranged another—all the mystery reconciles
throw away your obsessions because no means no.

FARCE

my flock comes and goes like the fever
and he is a herding dog who keeps running
with a sickness that never seems to stop or retreat
entangled by the wind, aged fast as a piece of bacon
yet the lambs are still hypnotised and confused by the projection of good behaviour
[hypnosis comes from years of ideological domestication and modification
confusion is the fodder of media cultures—they are bred and stuffed]
good boy. My kin and kind have the same colour, the same face, and even taste the same
brother to brother. It is all about impulsive copying and pasting with no moral needed
the weird thing is he just needs to show up, run naked, and voila! —a buffet is served
running through a paddy field where the sunlight leaves its abusive mark with yellow ease
there is never a shortage of good animals on a farm where desire has been trained, traded
and there is the dog who thinks he's a big deal in the market. He could not stop browsing
he thinks he's rich by favoured. He does not know he is chasing after an absurd dream
a silly recipe by a fetishy chef, with yeast and cumin that he fails to season it with.

CAPUT MORTUUM

Again, the past is in the present tense
If only my pains meant something to you—
The message was sharp and clear. Scarlet tinted the screen.

You are happy then. That your success at cutting a scene of attention: the worst kind
From your one way vengeance, I never forgive you. By dissecting me simultaneously,
We are in this rehearsal together. This ship of carving marks on flesh, replaced in flames.

Calls the emergency, you get to look after, but I was never the same. Remain broken
It is not news to you: this familiar circle dances on fire, acting intense to be present.
I am still working on myself, as trauma is transmutation in me. Are you feeling rewarding?
It hurts every day everywhere.

EVERYDAY LIKENESS
(WATCHING TOOTHPASTE GOING DOWN THE SINK)

Witnessing
death
it's hard
to be alive
like
toothpaste
on ceramic
hoarsely
fingers
slaying
greasy life
digging through
solid death
afterwards
I have
nothing to say
you have
nothing to do
afterwards
nothing happens
rewind
we lost
our lips

lips lost
in a busy street
skinny
&
secular
wet with scum
rotten pages
from newspapers
what's happening?
fuck we hate when that happens
we reckon
words dying
means
language dies
but
something is still alive
hard, like
a wall against which
it leans
on ceramics
reflective
&
thousands of lip balms
&
repeatedly brushing rhymes

E
V
E
R
Y
D
A
Y
L
I
K
E
N
E
S
S
S
Q
U
E
E
Z
E
S
M
E
H
A
R
D

like plastic items
slimy
&
sensual
shattered by feet
mottled leaves decaying
humbly
into uselessness
we found
this hour is deadly
who relives their lives
who cares
we know we don't
nor you nor them
nor us
it's better to be dead
like the best day
you ever had
no more brushing
happy days

ELEGY: THE DAY THE BUDGIE FLEW AWAY

You looked at me as if I were a ghost
one that would not go away—snake wrapped around the staff
for I died of some reluctant desire but you have seen too many melodramas

Under the gas-lamp I look at you in the mirror and all my speculations
and tricks are now exposed and expired and therefore it's insignificant

The type of you that is apathetic, insensible, unmoved
such a temptation you hold
such an incorrigible brat I am clinging to you

Let me erect and twitch in the whites of your eyes *Humiliate*
form deceased and be revisited—or you have never known me

THE FINEST BATOR

as I imagine having a circle jerk with Ashbery, Gunn, Morgan, O'Hara and Rimbaud

Exchanging seeds and dreams, passing on spits and desires,
To meet the eye or the hand that touches them. Gather round, soul's splashing!

Raging ballads, gentle bruises, all
Soaked and blended in a rug of woe and weal,
The iridescent arrangements. O how tall,
As if the world itself were at our heel.

Swollen wildlife, join the illuminated circuit of unleashing,
Word's miracles, as if they're heaven-sent bridges,
And still the vagabond beast's mystery, ever profound,
Defies all attempts to capture its heat and sound.

Underbelly areas, or shelves of self, sculpted with such care,
The body a reinforcer, the wood awakened by the act of art,
The resonance of past, present, reminiscing everywhere,
A renaissance of views and painters, young hearts throbbing, and meat's creating

INTERLUDE: AUROCHS

Your death excites and turns me on,
Between us: no distant hill, no loads wasted.
Sniff it. Take a grip on life, rebel against flaccidity.
Eat it. Let it flourish, with all of history's angelic vastness.

An ardour or jeopardy, a tangled parody they lay,
Tickling a forbidden itch, edging
Towards the brink, unable to sway.
Erased spectator's force it feeds, an insatiable thirst,
A serried page that burns, growing
You cannot exhaust, for the years of being ghosts.

We still exist, for the horny sake of grabbing onto
The inmost, hardest, best of the softest, star matters.

back here once more. Making promises
business as usual. Time to shine
takes a careful ritual, breathes deep
as in a shrine, to be blessed for life
beg for a drop of water, pole or cork
and a million secrets about men
crushed. Compacting this little world
is mandatory as a rosebud. Greatest uprising
breeds into the familiar darkness of emotions
Lazarus found himself here hesitating
return to the sky, going back to one root
realm's crowded and land's bared
nature and I are weak. Behind doors
that something was none other
than farewell's practice
the bells of it all.

NOTHING OLD
(After *Happy Together*)

These rains are threatened by the wind and under pressure, forced to let go
with resultant stories falling in droves, drenching a man with nothing to do.

A lucky guy like him, happy and roaming in the streetlight of nature, lighter than ever
longing for actual contact and, occasionally, romantic conjecture that is unproven.

Why don't we start all over again? He regrets it after a specific date
but love doesn't vapour into water. Even starting over will be vague.

Those days and nights of struggling, waiting for clear weather to show its mercy
to dry out old dreams of the past, leaving behind a dense carcass of bed mites.

Just to let us sleep through dusty turbulence, be odd, toasty warm and safely together
one time only—until next time and, lo and behold, see you at the waterfall, sincerely.

STRAIGHT AND CURVED
(After *Decision to Leave*)

Just the opposite, you came from the mountains, and I crossed the sea
By accident, we hit, lost and found. As the monument fell and the liquid boils
A volcano rages out and builds a treacherous island, with jealousy ready to stir the plot

Will you think of me? Rewind the breathing sound and an image of jellyfish before sleep
Will you let me sink in? It's harder to remember than grieve, leaving midnight's violence.
But your hugs were too warm, too cruel, like tiny hands that can't wash away angry blood.

Just as well apart. We may just as well happen to meet halfway
Sealife swallowed by lava, missing, like a small sandy hill at a tide rise
And then we woke up, and it became clear that loving was the biggest mistake

AT FIVE AM

Two bodies still intertwined like a chain stitch,
They had partied like migrating animals, wild and unrefined,
From the West Coast to East London, we tapped and coupled—
Our collarbones formed the Bosphorus bridge,
With eyes dangerous and blue as the Irish sea.

Under heavy rain, we traded goods and taxes,
Exploiting icy bed sheets, locking and pressing,
So hard that we became one distinct invention,
A not-so-heavy shell that two snails sheltered in, slowly warming up.

It's crazy how bitter weather played a big part in this sweet, minor encounter,
Where a 50-year-old spoiled prince is dozed,
Waiting for a thunderous morning alarm that's overdue,
Delayed from five minutes to five more centuries, not a care to hour and where.

I squeezed you tight, my muscles flexed, and you like it,
Compressing 5,437 miles of distance into one mighty craic, as you wanted.
Yet the time is up and the sun is out, so bright—totally burnt out,
The water dried up, and spilled salt, moon deleted,
Leaving only foam and bubbles, and so you disappeared.

STAY RIGID, STAY ALIVE

lust in the woods
sat on a figgy dildo
I keep my promises, as do you

flush of manhood
carved on me first
giving spit and nuts, penetrating

the goat bumps into Pinocchio
we swing the land as a bed. Shaft upwards—
whose lover continues to guide the way
throbbing commitment keeps a twink forever young.

REFLECTION

hence the moonlight wavers
bounces through grimy panes
quietly implying, enshrouding
drenching a half-splitting monstera

the unsettling glow is condescending
cutting green stripes at assembling
scars, proving of the body's remembrance—
thirst. The urge to wrestle with the nightmarish.

all askew, feels off-kilter as the air thickens
brooding turns even a streetlight powerless
turn away from untamed plants' dazzle and fusses
for envying their feet are always down to earth

addressing (self-help) aerated roots and rusted iron
nature sows divisions, so do humans
many moons have floated in and out of words and water
only to be cratered and become forlorn of one night's mortal.

CHRYSANTHEMUM BY HIS SIDE

Like all seeds that evolve into all varieties of thick and thin
He also carries in his body a garden: a good land in closeted
Amid the strict laws of patriarchy, one's fortunate enough to find
And rest a little bit in a warm fountain to preserve secret genesis
Though at times, the suffering comes with such force and speed
That the garden loses its varying colours, exposed to pressures

For real. The vast black and white flower tattooed on his waist resembles a supernova
Which once had its own glorious garden: a delicate vase destroyed by depression
Still warning of the gardener who planted the flowers and the blossoms that were cared for
The odds are that they both lean on each other, which makes it an even matter
Luck. Probability. Suspended. Because the weather is in stalemate most of the time
Trapped on the threshold, the door opened by death brings the descent of fall.

They are waiting for a big arrival. Enough pabulum and space for the roots to breathe
The fresh light of day after a shower soothed the shoot and entrenched: a motherland born
Washing away those dried ink stains and caked blood droplets. In embryo,
His body becomes a habitat. A rhizome, the branched and lobed shapes are profound
More revive than many living zombies. Then the years of picking and trampling abuse
Only to levitate the feathery decoration of his corpse, for it is heavier than the earth.

SUNDAY TOWER HAMLETS CEMETERY PARK, 2021

Pretended not to notice
And crept up to your neck
I smell the soft ends of your morning hair—
Vaporised summer fruits.

Ego leaps heavily from
Physical walls and ceilings
Through the clouds overhead—
Land on decayed bushes down under.

You tried on my sunnies
But cannot see what I see
The fathomless transparency of an unrequited crush—
On my eyes, as you oxidise me.

Infinitely we are close
And distant—close to me
Like the white plane that day
Marks—a big star you are—extraordinary.

TO SAY AYE

The aloe of your ver
Sweetens my misery
A sticky name echoes history distantly—we could be a portmanteau.

Tremendous hot air encroaches and ignites me from your calling
Shivers a breath which begins a solitaire game of unmeaning
At least nature seems to have had a face of its own. Travelling

To have tattered volcanic rocks swallow a white sand beach
Shown that I was once brave enough to burn, only to immerse—
Æt the sole bottom of your versæ.

THREE ISLANDS AND HUNTER IN AN AUTOBIOGRAPHY

Suddenly the endless sea of black was filled with a solitary blue light bulb
From that day on, the tides began to attack inland in the darkness.
The trainee hunter feels carsick and leans against the window
Staring blearily at the greenery, hoping and calling for banishment.
Driving from the mountains to the beach airport, even the memories start moving
Landing on another hunting ground, he was already disoriented

The winter there made him the prey of the disoriented.
He found a cabin in the woods, but inside was just a broken light bulb.
"I need a solid axe," he thought, trying to survive in this condition of fast-moving
Weapons, food, clothing, and a few diversions to pass the time in the darkness
Waiting to pocket all these, so full that the corner of his bandana leaked out, a banishment!
"All the island's encapsulated," he sighed after closing the window

The young hunter immerses himself in self-learning, opening every window
Grains of unfailing finish his eyes as if time had been lit up by a light bulb
Delicate words and pixels have been dismantled in the darkness
Covered with scars and tears; it seems he came into this world with banishment
And so, he carried the weight of history and is disoriented.
The wind and the rain may blow and wash away the erasable ones, but the water is moving

And water is everywhere and this continent has stopped moving.
Be water, and thus he swims. As the trajectory became appealing, he opened the window
Pop on a transcontinental train and worry-free about being disoriented.
As this metal dragon trespasses into Uluru, tension shows in the blinking light bulb
The sporadic shadow of silent trees and boulders plunged into darkness
He finally reaches the graduation in rapture and he enjoys self-banishment.

Like a boomerang, hunter on an island again, the fate of self-imposed banishment
No awkwardness: he gets used to being disoriented.
Sculptures are plants growing up in their niche. That's how you fix a light bulb—
Adapting different homes, exercising mental, social, and natural compatibility by moving
In a music video, vibing, sitting in a bus next to the window
A speed bump goes all the way out of the youth of darkness

Remember? Those invisible aches and pains haunted him in phantom darkness
Sly Mephisto waiting behind as a spider, left echoing in the banishment
He got a buzzcut—it reminded the hunter of a humming song: very moving
Like a bush fire that can't be put out. Slowly, he was dazed and a little disoriented
The dreams we had and the trace of the people before us will break the invisible window
On all the islands, sheltering him as the rounded overhead light bulb

Turn on the darkness. Outline the silhouette of the light bulb,
There goes self-banishment, forever circulating and moving
The parable: when disoriented travellers look up, they long to see their home's window.

HOLDING ON

Did I graduate
        Again with a degree of full scars
Healing, pilling skins of memory to aerial years
        Was I mourning
Full-time carrying a bodily hearse

Hold the gust objectively
        Rotating in profound orbits
You may come as a callous lover falling into dating fields
        Wild grass I lay on to embrace gravity in sorrows

Did the sun go
        Dawn, down, boulders done by erosions, thus colourless
Hearsay eagles tear up headstrong creatures who like us
        Am I capable of being lovable? Where the ghost of peach blossom land is
Sneezing milky stardust awaits

NOTES
AND ACKNOWLEDGEMENTS

Silver Spine speaks to Jean Genet, was first published in a pamphlet 'Reaching for the Horizon', by RCA Q.U.E.E.R. Society 2021.

Hunter For Ghost speaks to Arthur Rimbaud and 兔儿神 Tu'er Shen, a Chinese folk tale patron deity of homosexual love.

Silver Spine, Hunter For Ghost, and Boy were written in my last year at the Royal College of Art, and first appeared as 'Handkerchief Poems' in a mixed-media installation as part of my graduate degree show piece at MA Sculpture 2021: Proxy, in Cromwell Place, London.

In Ode On Topophilia, 'Topophilia' was coined and studied by humanistic geographer Yi-Fu Tuan.

In Three Desiring-Machines, Eros is after Anne Carson's 'Eros the Bittersweet', the Queen is Sappho, and 'colder than death' was borrow from Rainer Werner Fassbinder's 1969 film 'Love is Colder Than Death', which was first titled Kälter als der Tod (Colder than death).

In Later That Night, 'Lola' was a character borrowed from 'Run Lola Run', a 1998 film directed by Tom Tykwer.

In A Greedy Life, 'pragmatic and kinetic' is a reference from John Ashbery's 'The System'.

In It's Sexy, 'Our Lady of the Flowers' was borrowed from Jean Genet's novel of the same title.

In Trash Talking, 'heterotopia' and 'panopticon' are concepts explored and elaborated by Michel Foucault. 'I should put on my armour of ego' is an alter lyric from Arthur Rimbaud's 'A Season in Hell'.

In Three Fashionable Boyfriends, the shop is linked to SOPHIE's song 'Faceshopping'. 'Love me longer or love me not' alters a lyric from Lana Del Rey's song 'Happiness is a butterfly', 'Is the bus still running' is a reference from RuPaul's drag race.

In Farce, 'brother to brother' is a reference from 'Tongues Untied', a 1989 documentary directed by Marlon Riggs, and the words were written by Joseph Beam.

Caput Mortuum and Everyday Likeness contain suicidal thoughts. **Help is available**: call Samaritans at **116 123**, SMS text **SHOUT** to **85258**.

Elegy: The Day The Budgie Flew Away and the music score was made for a one-minute short film, as part of the Triage, a collaborative project between The Royal College of Art Sculpture Program and The Old Operating Theatre during the 2021 lockdown. First inspired by Hervé Guibert's novel 'To the Friend Who Did Not Save My Life', translated by Linda Coverdale. Also Gary Fisher's journals from his book 'Gary in your pocket', and Glenn Gould's performance of Bach's 'Goldberg Variations, BWV 988'. Thanks to Graham Hudson for organising the project.

The Finest Bator is after John Ashbery, Thom Gunn, Edwin Morgan, Frank O'Hara, Arthur Rimbaud, and many more. The 'heaven-sent bridges' also linked to Hart Crane's 'The Bridge'.

Captain of The Departure Department is written after the Tom of Finland Art & Culture Festival 2022, thanks to Durk Dehner for his kind words, Laurie and the Ridley Road Project Space for getting me involved. Laurie, Joe, Prem, George, you are phenomenal.

Nothing Old is after 'Happy Together', a 1997 film directed by Wong Kar-wai.
Straight And Curved is after 'Decision to Leave', a 2022 film directed by Park Chan-wook.

Reflection speaks to Pai Hsien-yung's novel 'Crystal Boys'.

'Only Fools Despair' and 'Chrysanthemum by His Side' is for B. 'Inner Canthal Region Eye Cream' is for E. 'Fall Hard, Fall Fast' is for Melbourne. 'Farce' is with thanks to William. 'Verse On A Vanishing Act' and 'To Say Aye' is for A.

Three Islands And Hunter In An Autobiography was first inspired by Elizabeth Bishop's 'One Art'. The 'humming song' is Lorde's 'Buzzcut Season'.

Thank you especially to these artists and figures, for their works and marks, being hunted down by me and transforming me into a hunter like them.

Many Thanks to Jamie Lee for all his editorial input.

J. William James for proofreading.

Conor Donlon for all his support.

Daniel Faltys for the delicate graphic design.

Sarah Staton — my RCA tutor, for all her support and for including me with the 'Handkerchief Poems (Silver Spine, Hunter For Ghost, Boy)' in the group show 'SupaStore Southside, Slingbacks and Sunshine' in South London Gallery 2021.

Tom Legg for his support and advice.

Anal House Meltdown for the hot, sweaty clubbing nights.

Thank you to my sisters, brothers, nephews, nieces, mother and father.
Please don't read this either. 我爱你们。

Vers Aloe
Deming Huang

First published in 2023
by Overwhelm Press

Printed by TJ Books Limited

Designed by Daniel Faltys

All artwork by Deming Huang

A CIP record for this book is available from the British Library

ISBN 978-1-7394394-0-8

www.overwhelmpress.com
info@overwhelmpress.com
@overwhelmpress

ISBN 978-1-7394394-0-8
9 781739 439408 >